Mommy's Milk

Is Going Bye-Bye!

Written and Illustrated by Marianna Estrada

Written and illustrated by Marianna Estrada on March 1, 2017.

Self published April 7, 2019.

ISBN: 978-0-692-05063-7

For Abuela and Abuelo:
I am me because of you. Your values are my
values. I think of you both every day.

For my handsome Bubby and
pretty Wittle Woo:
I treasure you and love you.
Thanks to God, for sending you to me.
I'm glad you're the ones I got.
From the moment you started life,
I started living.

And, for tired mommies everywhere.
Hang in there!

Mommy says at first I was so little that I had to live in her tummy until I grew bigger.

On the day I was big enough,
I was born!

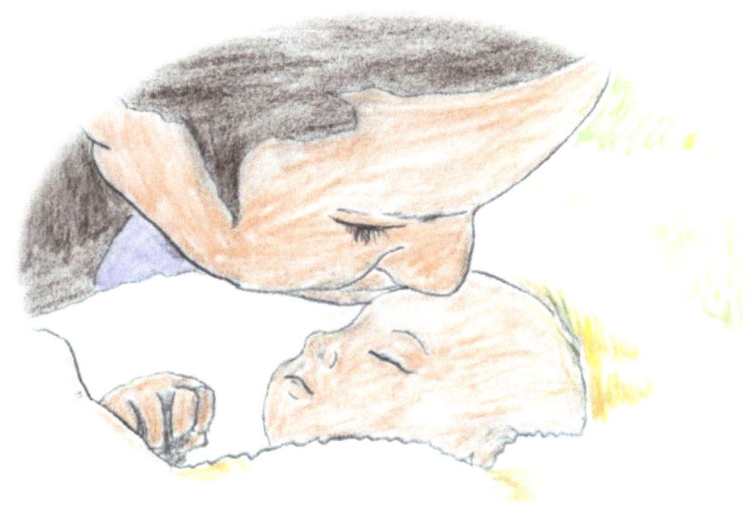

I was so little...

I could fit into a Christmas stocking!

Mommy says at first
I was so little,

I couldn't eat food. I could only
drink Mommy's milk from my
Mommy's body.

Mommy's milk was so good for me, that I grew bigger and stronger.

Soon, I could sit up all by myself!
I like my Mommy's milk!

I crawled,

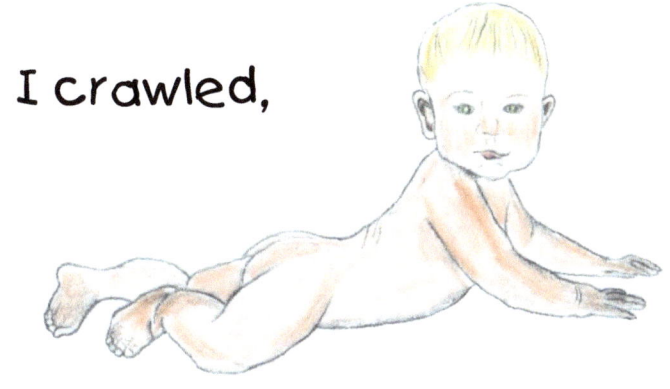

then I could stand-up, and then I walked, all by myself!

As I got bigger,

                I could eat food!

Mommy says now that I am a big toddler, Mommy's milk is going to go bye-bye because I don't need it anymore.

I'm sad that when I go nursies, there's hardly any milk. But, I'm happy when I'm eating good food!

Mommy says now it's my job to put food in my tummy. I can drink milk from the fridge, like co-co milk, goatie milk and moo cow's milk!

I can eat meat, fruit, veggies, and other good food, too.

And, cake-cake! And, ice cream!

Mmmmm!

I don't need Mommy's milk anymore, but I still want it.

When I want to go nursies, Mommy says I can do other fun stuff so I will be happy-- like being held by Mommy.

I love Mommy and she loves me.

I can go swingies at the park with Horsie,

or play with my dollies.

I can color with my crayons,

or just hang out with my sippy cup full of milk.

I can wear a funny wig, or just hang out with my big Bubby.

I love my Bubby and he loves me.

Sometimes, Daddy takes me sleddies in the snow, or we go hikies in the desert.

I love Daddy and he loves me!

I know even though Mommy's milk is going bye-bye, I have lots of good food and fridge milk to drink.

I know that I can do lots of things to feel happy.

And, I know that I am loved!

About the Author and Artist

Marianna Estrada has a bachelor's degree in Mass Communications and has worked as a reporter, a photographer, and an associate editor of a small-town newspaper. She is an avid reader, loves the outdoors, and is very interested in holistic nutrition and the Paleo lifestyle. She received a degree in Gourmet Cooking and Catering and loves to cook. She was up nursing her own daughter every night for two years and two months before she decided to write this book. She also has a handsome teenage son who has kept her up at night with worry. This is her first book.

www.ingramcontent.com/pod-product-compliance
Lightning Source LLC
Chambersburg PA
CBHW041234040426
42444CB00002B/165